CONTENTS

DEALING WITH PROBLEM CLIENTS

Building Fences Around Friendly Monsters

Nathan Ingram

ISBN: 978-1-949289-04-6

Published by Peculiar Productions, LLC

FOREWORD

I read this book in 54 minutes. I lost 1,664 hours to not having read it sooner. But that's just a guess. It's probably more.

I met Nathan at WordCamp Denver 2016. He was helping us stamp the WP logo onto swag boxes. As an Organizer, he was just another guy I met in passing. High five. Thanks for the help.

My staff saw his talk, *"Dealing with Problem Clients."* They insisted we make time to watch it together. That was June. We got around to watching it in December.

I paused it halfway through and exclaimed:

"We're hiring Nathan!"

"What for?"

"To be our business coach!"

"Does he even do coaching?"

"Doesn't matter! We're hiring him."

"Maybe we should finish watching the video first..."

We had no fences. No contracts. No checklists. No peace of mind. No control.

We were flying by the seat of our pants with no instruments. Or stick. Or parachute. Or windshield.

The fences went up slowly. We did hire Nathan. Obliterating my 1 Coach for 1 Year rule, he's still our coach 25 months later. We're still doing good work together. There's a lot left to do.

I like the view from my fenced dominion. Every now and then one of the monsters Kilroys over the fence. We chat like Tim and Wilson.

Fences make great clients.

Gordon Seirup
Copper Leaf Creative

INTRODUCTION

I love freelancers. My calling is to help WordPress business owners thrive. I was bitten by the entrepreneurial bug in my early 20s. And 25 years later, I'm still at it. There are two reasons why…

First, as a person of faith, I believe that every human being is wired in a unique way to make a difference in the world. The goal is to couple the way you're wired with an occupation that can generate the revenue to support your life. When you find that sweet spot, it's a powerful thing.

Second, there is a remarkable freedom that comes from owning your own business and being in control of your own priorities. There is no such thing as a secure corporate job any more. Repeatedly, I've seen people close to me experience long periods of unemployment and struggle because of a decision to downsize made at a boardroom table.

Some say being a business owner or a freelancer is risky. Perhaps. But I'd much rather rise and fall on my own work than be at the mercy of behind-closed-doors corporate decisions.

Owning your own business allows you to support your lifestyle by doing what you love to do, while offering the freedom to invest time in your family and other priorities. It's not easy, but the payoff is worth it!

I started freelancing when I was in college. I was doing IT consulting in those days, working with my next-door neighbor who was the quintessential entrepreneur. I went from selling computers at Radio Shack to working for lawyers and other small businesses in the afternoons after class.

When I graduated from college, I worked in the nonprofit sector for almost 20 years. The organizations I served were small. And if you know anything about the nonprofit world, you won't be shocked when I tell you that I wasn't making very much money doing it. But since I had a lucrative freelance business alongside, I could work as my schedule allowed and earn money to make ends meet.

Over that 20 years, I worked in my freelance business at varying percentages of my time.

Sometimes I'd be very part time, 10 hours or less a week. Other times, I'd be nearly full-time depending on what the organization I was working for could afford. But regardless, I was building a financial engine that allowed me to continue the important work I was doing in the nonprofit world.

Several years ago, I left the nonprofit world and began focusing full-time on business, working with clients to build websites and serving as a coach and educator for freelancers and business owners in the WordPress space. It has been my privilege to help my coaching clients create an efficient business that can power their life priorities, whatever they might be at a given time. Whether your goal is to work full time as a primary bread winner, work part-time just to help make ends meet, or anywhere in between, creating an efficient business is important. And the benefits are many.

But it's not easy. There are plenty of problems that complicate the lives of business owners.

I've talked to WordPress business owners across the country and around the world. And many are just one more bad client away from throwing in the towel. And it's a shame. Because most client problems are fixable with systems and processes.

That's why I wrote this book.

Dealing with Problem Clients is one of the most popular talks I've given at WordCamps around the country. It always seems to resonate with the audience because we've all struggled with difficult clients. And we're all looking for ways to help prevent those experiences from happening again.

This book is presented in two parts.

The first part is fiction. A series of fables, if you will. It's a set of four stories about WordPress freelancers who encounter "Friendly Monsters," problem clients that are causing trouble in their lives and businesses. Chances are, you'll see yourself in one of these characters or situations as you watch them handle the problem with input from a business coach and others.

The second part is nonfiction. It explains the "Four Fences," essential systems and structures that must be present in your business in order to keep problem clients contained. In this section, I offer lots of specific tips, but you'll find the principles are broad enough to be applied in many creative ways to your business.

It is my sincere hope that you'll find great value in this book, and that it plays a helpful role in your growth as a business owner.

PART ONE:

FRIENDLY MONSTERS

THE QUESTION MARK

"Three hours," Theresa said to herself as she walked out of the coffee shop and toward her car. "I've been in there for three hours. I can't believe it."

It started innocently enough. The week before, she had been at her gym in a spin class and struck up a conversation with the woman on the stationary bike next to her. Her new friend was starting a business selling handmade jewelry, and as soon as she heard that Theresa was a web designer, she was immediately full of excitement and questions.

"Do you think my jewelry would sell?"

"How should I handle shipping?"

"Do you think Facebook ads are really worth it?"

Theresa was just getting started in her web design business as well, but she wasn't about to let her new friend find that out. Although she was new to freelancing, Theresa was no stranger to the web. Earning a degree in marketing, she was a rising star at her previous job – a large local advertising agency that handled websites and digital marketing for an assortment of clients.

Theresa had started working for the agency right out of college. She married about a year later and had two children over the next four. As much as she loved her work, her priorities began to change. Family had always been important to her, so she made the tough decision to trade the long hours she was working at the agency for caring for her children full time.

That was six years ago. As her children grew, so did her free time. Theresa was never one for idleness, so when her youngest started preschool, she started freelancing. She was doing pretty well, building a website here and there for friends of friends and a few local businesses.

She wasn't trying to build an agency. She wasn't even trying to work full time. She was working to bring in some extra money to make things easier each month, and maybe even save enough to pay cash for a trip to Disney later that year. With those goals as the yardstick, she was doing quite well.

"Your business is the engine that powers your lifestyle," her business coach Jason had told her a few months earlier. "Don't get caught up measuring yourself against others, just know whether or not your business is accomplishing its purpose for your life."

It was excellent advice that was starting to set her free from the massive inferiority complex she had quietly developed in the early days of her business. But as she walked out of the Starbucks that day, she was feeling utterly defeated. "Three hours!" She tossed her arms halfway into the air and shook her head with exasperation as she reached her car.

It was the third Tuesday of the month, so it was time for her one on one coaching call with Jason. Jason was a seasoned web developer who had been working with clients for almost 25 years. He loved creating systems and processes, but even more than that, he loved helping freelancers optimize their businesses to support their priorities. Investing some money in coaching was one of the best things Theresa had ever done.

By the time she got home and connected to the video call, she was almost late. And as soon as Jason saw her on the screen, he knew she was frustrated.

"So... what's going on today?" he asked with a grin. Theresa was high energy, and Jason always enjoyed their conversations.

"I just had the worst meeting of my life." Theresa started in, explaining how she'd met the client at a spin class and scheduled the one-hour-turned-three meeting at the coffee shop.

"So, tell me what happened in the meeting."

"It all started out pretty normally. We got our coffee and started talking small talk. But I could never seem to change the subject to her website. We talked about her kids, her dog, her husband's motorcycle, her dog again... I swear if I had to hear one more story about that Bichon Frise, I was going to scream."

"So how long did that go on?"

"More than a half hour! At first, I was just trying to develop a connection, but she just wouldn't shut up. I've never seen anything like it. We were 45 minutes in before we even really started talking about her business at all."

"Sounds like something that would drive me crazy too. Tell me what happened when you finally got around to the business. What did you ask her? How did she respond?"

"That's the thing. I didn't get many questions in at all. And it seemed like every time I'd ask her a question. She'd ask me three right back. She'd bounce from thing to thing. One minute she'd be talking about sales tax, and as I'd start digging into that a little, she'd change the subject to email marketing. I was getting dizzy."

"I don't blame you. Sounds like you just met

a Question Mark."

"A Question Mark?"

"Yep, a question mark is a client who loves to ask questions. They have no idea what they really want. They have no goals, no budget. They love to talk. They love to dream. And they will suck your life away if you let them."

"That's exactly what happened to me today. I just lost three hours. I'm no closer to closing the deal, and I'm exhausted."

"I'm not surprised. Question Marks are classic time wasters. What happened when you started talking price?"

"We never got there. I pretty much just answered one question after another. When I saw what time it was, we just planned to talk again later since I had to leave to do our call."

"OK, let's talk about how to handle these kinds of clients. When you deal with a Question Mark, you have to control the conversation. Do you have an intake form?"

"An intake form, meaning..."

"Just a list of questions that you ask every client when you meet with them for the first time."

"Oh, I have a list of things in my mind. But

not an official list I guess."

"That's where you start. You want to make a list of questions that you're going to ask every client, every project, every time. That way when you sit down with them, you have a plan. You set the agenda."

"I guess I just like the conversation to happen organically."

"I can understand that. A list doesn't mean it can't be natural. But you're spending your time to meet with the client, and you really have to think about it that way. What's your hourly rate?"

"75 dollars per hour."

"We're going to need to talk about that. It's not enough. But staying on topic... you just spent 3 hours with this client. How much money did you spend? And I mean based on your hourly rate, not how much the coffee cost."

"Well, I guess I spent $225." A lump was rising in Theresa's throat.

"Yep, $225. And did the client hire you?"

"No."

"Is she close to hiring you?"

"I don't think so. I don't even know if she has the money to spend. You know, these kinds of clients didn't bother me as much when I was working for the agency. I got paid my salary regardless. But now, I just can't afford to waste this kind of time."

"Right. That's why you need a set list of questions that you ask, and at the beginning of the meeting you ask for the potential client's permission to walk down your list so that you make sure you cover all the details you need so that you can both use the time most efficiently."

"I like the sound of that."

"That way you're not bullying the conversation. You've asked and received permission to run the meeting. And a good client will be impressed with your approach. If they push back on you, it's a red flag."

"That makes a lot of sense."

"Now let me let you in on a little secret I learned a long time ago about the Question Mark."

"I'm all ears."

"The best way to deal with a Question Mark is with a Dollar Sign."

"What?"

"Yep. As soon as I realize I'm dealing with a Question Mark, I immediately shift the conversation to price. You want to get to price as quickly as possible and help them see that your answers to their questions have value. It's all about commitment. You have to get some kind of financial commitment from a Question Mark quickly. Otherwise they'll monopolize your time with questions and dreams."

"So, you don't answer any questions?"

"Oh sure, I'll answer questions. But you have to keep in mind what the purpose of the first meeting with the client is all about. You're there to get enough information to write a proposal. You're not there to be a sounding board for the client's hopes and dreams. I'll answer the questions that help us move toward the goal of getting all that information. But mostly I'm going to be the one asking the questions."

"So, what kinds of questions will you answer?"

"Here's a good rule of thumb… WHAT questions tend to be informational. Those are questions I'll usually answer, at least in short. But HOW questions tend to start getting into intellectual property. Those have answers that they'll usually need to pay for. Obviously, you don't want to be a jerk about it. I'll joke about it with them a lot of times. 'Hey, I'll be happy to answer that question, but I'll need to send you an invoice afterward. Ha-ha-ha.' That kind of thing."

"OK, now I follow you. That approach sure would have made my meeting today a lot more productive."

"For sure. Now sometimes you won't be able to get all the answers to the questions you need in the first meeting. You may step into some deep water you don't understand. The client may not have all the answers to the questions you're asking. And that's ok. When you hit that kind of situation, it's time for a discovery phase or a consulting agreement of some kind."

"I've heard of those, but I've never used one. How does it work."

"Don't overthink it. It's really pretty simple. Think of it like any other project. You have a deliverable and a price. Your deliverable (the scope of work) is to provide answers to the questions you list out. And there's a price attached to those answers which you'll supply in a report. I like to explain it to the client as a good test of whether working together for the long haul is a good fit. I'll help them find the answers they need and, if at the end of that process, we both feel good about continuing, we move forward. If not, they have an actionable document that they can use to hire their next web professional."

"Got it. That does sound pretty simple."

"So, what's your next step?"

"I'm going to create a list of questions to use for all my initial client meetings."

"What about Ms. Question Mark?"

"I'm not sure I can take another meeting like that. I think I may just not pursue it and see if she ever decides to call me again. Even if she does, I'm not sure she's going to be someone I want to work with long-term."

"Smart. Trust your gut. And don't be afraid to say no to a client. Bad clients always cost you more in mental and emotional capital than you'll ever make from them in real dollars."

"I couldn't agree more."

THE INVISIBLE MAN

"Wow!" Carlos said with wide eyes as he set his coffee mug slowly back on the counter. "That is some of the best coffee I've ever had."

"Incredible, isn't it?" James agreed. "It was roasted right in front of me three days ago by the farmer himself."

Carlos was a self-proclaimed coffee snob (and proud of it). He relished drinking the three pounds of the freshly roasted beans that James had brought back from a church mission trip to Guatemala. Carlos was the youth pastor of the small congregation, and several of his students had joined James for the trip over Christmas break.

"Well, now that I've fed your addiction, I'll let you get back at it," James said as he stood and walked toward the door of the church office.

"Thanks, man! See you this weekend." Carlos closed the door behind him and began thinking about the day ahead. In addition to serving the junior and senior high school students of Living Hope Church as their youth pastor, Carlos had a small but growing web development business.

A few years earlier, Carlos wanted a great website for Living Hope so that families with teenagers could more easily connect with the congregation. But there was no budget in the small church to pay for a professional. They could barely pay him a livable salary, even for a single guy in his mid-20s. Carlos had always had an affinity for technology, so he decided he'd just learn to do it himself.

Over the next few months, he learned the basics of HTML and CSS. And when he discovered WordPress, it all came together. He cobbled together a website from themes and plugins that others had recommended. His first effort wasn't the best, but it worked. And as he modified it in the coming months, he honed his skills as well.

A year later, he launched the second version of the Living Hope website, and it was a success. Not only did it work well, but it also looked professional. Carlos was proud, and others began to notice his work.

Not long after, he received a call from a friend who was a Youth Pastor in a small church in a neighboring town. They had seen Carlos' work and wanted to hire him to build their new website. That story repeated itself over and over until, three years later, Carlos had a dozen church and nonprofit organization websites under his belt and was even starting an ecommerce website for a local business.

His web business was perfect because it provided the flexibility to work in ministry and helped make ends meet. Plus, he was able to make far more in a part-time web business than he ever could have working hourly in retail.

Carlos knew that if he were going to build websites, there would be a steep learning curve in technology. He learned quickly. What he didn't anticipate was that the business side of things would be such a challenge as well. Carlos had always been good with people, but sometimes clients and their demands proved to be more than he could handle.

It was in the early days of his business when he'd met Jason. A mutual friend had introduced Jason as a business coach that he probably needed to meet. Carlos was just starting out and didn't have the money to hire a business coach. But Jason was helpful with free advice and checked in with Carlos every few months after their initial meeting.

"Remember, you don't have to know everything about web design," Jason told him. "None of us do. Do what you do best and find trustworthy partners for the rest."

Carlos listened to the advice.

As the business finally started to bring in decent money, Carlos invested in Jason's coaching officially. They started working one on one for a few months, and as the business continued to grow, Jason invited Carlos to join his coaching group.

The group was made up of five other freelance web developers scattered across the country, and Carlos felt right at home. During the monthly video call, each participant would bring an issue to the group that they needed help with, and the group would work the issue together as Jason moderated and offered insight.

It was incredibly effective. Not only was Carlos getting answers to the challenges in his own business, but the issues that others brought were either things he was also facing or things he knew he'd probably face in the future.

Occasionally he'd even have some wise suggestions for someone else's issue because he had dealt with it himself in the past. And that helped build his confidence.

"We're all cut from the same cloth," Jason would say. "There are no unique problems among web developers. The details might be a little different, but the principles are the same."

As Carlos closed the door to his office and turned toward his desk, he grinned. It wasn't just the French press of rich coffee that made him smile. It was Forum Day – the day each month his coaching group met to get help with their issues.

Carlos had a good issue for the group today.

The video call began with celebrations and updates. Jason was a firm believer in group members celebrating their business wins with people who could appreciate them. It was something Carlos appreciated. It was such a thrill to share the clever solution to a technical problem he'd find or to report on a proposal he'd closed with a new client. When he'd share his wins with friends, he'd often watch their eyes glaze over. In the group, he found his tribe, where everybody understood the difficulties, and everybody could appreciate the successes.

It was his turn, so Carlos began to unpack his issue. "A few months ago, I started working with a realtor to build a personal website."

There was an audible groan from a few of the group members.

"What's that about?" Carlos chuckled.

"Realtors and attorneys," Shawn said. "They're some of the hardest clients to work with." The others agreed. Shawn was a self-proclaimed country boy who had joined the group a few months earlier. He had a great sense of humor and a thick southern accent. Carlos liked him immediately.

"Anyway, I started working with this realtor," Carlos continued. "It's a fairly small website other than the need to include MLS listings. I've worked through all of that, but I'm having problems with the client himself. Things started off okay, but now it's like he disappeared on me."

"What do you mean?" asked Margot. Margot had started the group about the same time as Carlos. She was a retired junior high math teacher. Working with students, they had a lot in common.

"Well, I haven't heard from him in weeks. He isn't returning my calls or emails. And even before that, our communication wasn't very regular, to begin with. He's just a hard guy to get hold of."

"What were your first few contacts with him like?" asked Theresa who had worked with a handful of realtors in her agency position years earlier.

"Now that I think of it," Carlos pondered, "he's always been hard to reach. It took a whole string of emails back and forth to schedule our first meeting. And he was always so slow to respond. He kept having things come up. And then he even rescheduled the first meeting after we had planned. Good thing my schedule is pretty flexible."

"I worked with a client like that myself last year," Theresa responded. "It's like he was hot or cold. He was either super interested or completely absent. And I could never get him to return a phone call or an email."

"Carlos, it looks like you're dealing with an Invisible Man," Jason added. "Sounds like you may have been too, Theresa."

Both of them laughed.

Jason continued, "The Invisible Man is what I call a client who wants a website one day and then is nowhere to be found the next. What I've learned is that these kinds of clients are usually well-intentioned, but busy. They're professionals, like your realtor, or a small business owner who has a lot demands on her time. When you hear from them, it's because on that day the website is their top priority. But tomorrow, one of their other top priorities has taken their attention."

"So, what do you do in this situation?" Carlos asked.

"At the agency, we'd just put their project on pause until they were ready to pick it back up again," Theresa explained. "They'd already paid us the deposit. We'd just start working on projects for other clients."

"That's true," Jason agreed, "but the problem with these kinds of clients is that when they finally come back around again, they often have unreasonable demands. Like 'you've had three months to work on this, why isn't it finished yet?' Completely forgetting that for those three months you've been stalled because they haven't provided the content or the assets you need to complete the work."

Everybody nodded.

"This is when the Invisible Man becomes the Stealth Bomber," Jason joked. "He reappears out of thin air and drops bombs all over your world."

"So back to Carlos' question, what are you supposed to do in that kind of situation?" Shawn asked.

"Well, the first thing you need is to have clarity in your contract around what happens when a project is delayed by the client. They need to understand the project gets suspended if they don't communicate or provide assets. And when they're ready to start the project again, it has to go to the end of the pipeline of work you have at that time."

"Not only that," Jason continued, "but it also makes sense to put some boundaries around just how long a project can be suspended. In my experience, the longer a project goes, the more opportunities arise for misunderstandings."

"So, what's a good time frame?" Carlos asked,

"In my contract, I explain that if a client delays the project for more than 30 days, it is considered suspended," Jason answered. "At that time, in order to reactivate the project, the client will have to pay the balance due in full and supply any remaining assets needed to complete the work. And they go to the end of the line."

"But," Jason continued, "If 60 more days pass after the project was suspended, it is considered abandoned, and the client forfeits the deposit. We will give the client any work we've done to that point, of course, but the project is over."

"You're not messing around, are you?" Margot laughed.

"Well, I honestly got tired of having my workflow disrupted by clients who would disappear. It caused all kinds of stress in my personal life, and I just wasn't going to have it anymore."

Heads were nodding across the country on the video call.

"OK, so what do I do now that I'm working with an Invisible Man?" Carlos asked. "And I don't have anything in my contract like that to help me out."

"Well, that does make it more complicated," Jason replied.

"You can just leave well enough alone if you want," Margot suggested. "As Theresa said earlier, eventually the client will show up again. And you've gotten the deposit."

"I'd like to get paid for the rest of the project though," Carlos said. "I've done so much work getting things to the point they are now, not to mention setting up the MLS feed."

"Yeah, I can certainly see that," said Margot. "I'd want to get paid too."

Jason spoke up, "What I'd recommend is doing whatever you can to get a meeting with this client. In person if at all possible. You need to talk through what has the project stuck and how you can help him unstick it."

"Well, that part I know already. We need professional headshots, and we need marketing copy for the informational pages. It's not that much really."

"Do you know a photographer? A copywriter?" Jason asked.

"Yes, I know a couple of each," Carlos said. He had taken Jason's advice a few months earlier and started intentionally networking with other freelancers in the area to build his referral network.

"So why don't you take the initiative and get the client's permission to schedule with one of the photographers? Make sure that they can come to his office and make it all happen right there. Same goes for the copywriter. Get your client to plan 2 hours one afternoon with her and talk through the website copy you need like an interview. Then she can put the copy together for you."

"Yeah, that could actually work," Carlos agreed.

"Normally, you'd want to charge extra for this kind of project management service, but at this point, it's just about getting the project unstuck, done and launched," Jason added.

"Got it! I think I have some good action steps to take now. I'm going to add new language to my contract to deal with these things, and get this current client connected with my contacts so we can get the project out the door." Carlos was already feeling relieved.

"Anybody else have comments or suggestions?" Jason asked. "Great issue Carlos.

Make sure you keep us up to date on how it plays out."

"Definitely."

THE BOUNDARY BUSTER

"That's the last straw. It's really the last straw," Shawn thundered as he put his phone face down on the coffee table a little too hard.

"Come on honey, it's Christmas," his wife Terri chided from the other side of the room. "The kids are opening presents. Can't the business wait for a day?"

"Exactly. It's Christmas. And this... ahhem... person is demanding that I make some changes on her website." Shawn was fuming. "This is exactly why I got out of IT."

For years, Shawn had run a semi-successful IT business troubleshooting PCs and managing small office networks. Nothing complicated, but it was work that people needed, and he was someone they could rely on. And people loved Shawn, who was always ready with a smile or a funny story. He was just an uplifting guy to be around.

Shawn had been self-employed providing IT services since college. As he grew older, married, and had two kids, Shawn began to realize that the amount of time his business was consuming was eating into the time he needed to be spending with his family. And as his kids grew, he knew they would need more and more of his time.

It was a call from a pushy client three years earlier at his youngest daughter's 4th birthday party that had been the previous last straw for Shawn. On the other end of the phone was one of the partners of a small law firm, a man in his 60s who had been bypassed by the technological revolution. Even though Shawn explained that he was at his daughter's birthday party, his client demanded that he just take a few minutes to help him set up email on the new iPhone he bought. Surely it wouldn't take that long.

Shawn refused, and the client got angry and hung up the phone. The next day, he lost the account. That was the push he needed to renew his focus on learning how to build websites with WordPress, something he'd been dabbling with for a while.

Shawn had built a website for his business, and it wasn't a bad job. He enjoyed it, and he knew he could offer it as a service to his clients. More importantly, he figured he could probably control his time better and work more standard hours doing web design than he could working IT where he was essentially on-call 24/7.

He had put the idea on the back-burner because he was too busy with the services he was providing to worry about the services he wasn't. But that call, the birthday call, was the push he needed to make the change he knew was best.

Within a month, he hammered out a deal with another IT solopreneur to buy his business, his clients really, and used the money to live while he learned more about the web and worked on getting a new kind of client.

As part of the deal, his buyer had agreed to promote Shawn's web services to all his clients. It was an excellent fit and both their businesses grew.

But now it was Christmas. And this call from a client was triggering buried frustrations of the birthday call from years earlier.

"I'm not letting this happen again," Shawn insisted. "I'm not answering her until January. And if she leaves me, she leaves me. Ok, sorry about the interruption. Let's get back to the presents!"

Three days later, Jason was in his office catching up on email that had come in over the holidays. A Slack notification popped in. It was Shawn. "SOS – Have a minute?" Jason knew it had to be important.

"Sure, he typed. Let's do a quick call."

The Slack voice call connected quickly, and they were talking. Shawn explained what happened on Christmas with the demanding client. "I'm about to kick her to the curb. I don't care about the monthly retainer."

"Yeah, that's pretty ridiculous," Jason agreed. "But before you do anything rash, let's talk through it a bit. Why did she want you to make changes to her website on Christmas? Is she selling something? Or was there some kind of urgent need?"

"No, she was just working and wanted some changes made. Can you believe that? I mean, sure, work on Christmas if you want, but don't expect everybody else to. And don't make demands when people are trying to spend time with their families." Shawn was getting angry again just thinking about it. "She sent me 15 texts! 15!"

"Whoa, you're giving your clients your personal cell phone number? Ok, that's another conversation that we'll need to have later. But let's dig in on the client a little right now. Is this the first time she's made demands like that?"

"Nope, it started after our first call. She wanted to meet on a weeknight. And you know I usually don't work after 6 pm at the latest. Family time and all. But she insisted it was the only time she could meet, so I gave in. Then once I started to build her website, she could never talk during the day because she couldn't spend time on a side project at work. Ok, fair enough, but now all our calls have to be at night."

"I see a pattern unfolding."

"Oh, it gets worse my friend. She's a night owl. I'd wait days to get a response from her on an email and then she'd send a reply at 2 or 3 in the morning, which is fine. But then she'd email again around 10 am the next morning wondering if I'd had a chance to make the adjustment she wanted in the design."

"Shawn, you've got a Boundary Buster."

"So, you've got a name for this one too?" Shawn joked. He'd heard Jason talk about the Invisible Man and the Question Mark during group calls since he joined Jason's coaching group a few months earlier.

"Yep. And Boundary Busters are some of the worst. They have no respect for you, your time, or your family. They want what they want when they want it. And they have no qualms about pushing you hard to make it happen."

"The thing is, this lady is a life coach. I figured if anyone had it together, she did. And she's turned out to be one of the worst human beings I've ever dealt with in business."

Jason laughed, knowing full well the kind of people who were passing themselves off as coaches these days. "It's hard to be a good coach if you're selfish," he replied. "You genuinely have to be in it for the benefit of others if you're going to make a difference."

"Ok, Obi-Wan, how do I handle Ms. Boundary Buster?"

"Like I said, tricky one. You have to start early with these, or they're much harder to deal with because they set the tone early in the relationship. They're just bullies if you think about it. As soon as you sense a client is pushing against the boundaries you set, it's absolutely critical that you hold firm."

"Like taking those after-hours meetings. I knew I shouldn't have done that."

"Depends on the client. If it's an occasional exception, we can all live with that. But when you're being pushed and pushed and pushed, well at some point you just have to say stop."

"I wanted to text her the middle finger on Christmas morning. But I've just gone radio silent instead."

"Probably the better choice. You can catch a Boundary Buster early in the relationship by clearly communicating how and when you work, and watching how they react. You explain that you're available by phone and email during regular business hours. Never by text or, worse, some kind of social media messenger."

"Yeah, I made that mistake before. I became friends with a client on Facebook and he started messaging me there instead of emailing me. Really hard to communicate well that way and keep track of all the messages in different places."

"Exactly. So, when you explain your rules, and the client pushes back against what you're saying, you might be dealing with a Boundary Buster. Hold your ground unless there's a legitimate reason. And, again, you might need to bend your rules occasionally. But if they insist, you just tell them you're probably not the best fit for them. Or you can give them what I call the PITA surcharge."

"PITA?"

"Yep, Pain in the Asterisk."

"You're too kind."

"Probably, but I've marked up a client's proposal cost by 30-50% because I knew they were going to be hard to deal with. So, if I was going to work with them, the price was going to be worth it."

"So how do I fire this client? I'm done playing her games."

"Now that's a more complicated discussion. We've talked about a lot since you started with coaching, but I don't think we've gotten into your contract yet, have we? Do you have language that describes what happens when you want to separate from a client?"

"Unfortunately not."

"I see that a lot. It's a tricky situation, but it can get complicated quickly if you don't have good legal language to back you up. Especially when you're dealing with a problem client."

"I didn't think I'd need it. People usually love me."

"Well, you're a lovable guy," Jason laughed. "But listen, you don't have a contract for the good clients… you have it for the bad ones. And since you don't really know what kind of client you're dealing with, they all have to sign it. You know probably half the language in my contract is there because I had a problem and it wasn't covered there? I had to add it after the fact so that if I had a problem like that again, I'd be protected."

"Well, I guess I'm in good company then."

"The best, of course." They both laughed. "Do you think you can finish this project? Can you just get it done so you can turn the page?"

"Man, I don't know. I'd rather not have to deal with her at all anymore."

"I can appreciate that, but let me ask you this… what are the chances that she sues you if you decide to fire her under terms she doesn't like? And what are the chances she's going to agree to any terms you propose?"

"Yeah, I'm not sure. I wouldn't put anything past her at this point."

"Since you don't have this spelled out in your contract, you'd have to have a meeting of the minds on what separation looks like. Honestly, as hard as it is, it's probably going to be best for you to try to finish the scope of work you promised, get paid, and then move on with your life. Just consider it a learning experience."

"As much as I don't want to, you're probably right. I'll definitely have a better radar for this kind of situation next time, and I'm going to add separation language to my contract."

"What I'd suggest is that you make this your issue for the group call next week. I think everybody would learn from your experience and you might get some additional insight into your next steps. You'll also probably get some great samples of language for your contract from the other group members."

"Great idea! I'll do that for sure."

"Merry Christmas my friend, and Happy New Year."

"Same to you Obi-Wan. Oh, and I'm sending you a light saber for your birthday."

THE DRAMA QUEEN

Margot was late. And she was never late.

Jason stared at his screen, where his video conferencing software showed his face on one side and a black box on the other, waiting for Margot to join for their monthly one on one call.

Margot was a retired middle school teacher, who had somehow managed to survive teaching Pre-Algebra to 7th and 8th graders for 25 years. Two years earlier, and in the middle of a divorce, she'd had enough of childishness in her life, both from her students and from her soon-to-be ex-husband. It was time for a clean break, and she decided it was now or never.

Margot had always been the teacher who was on the cutting edge of technology in the classroom. She had been the first at her school to integrate computers into her classroom, make full use of a video projector, and dazzle her students with a smart board.

But it was her blog that really got attention. Margot started a WordPress blog for her students and parents that explained the concepts she was teaching in the classroom and even had videos of her working sample problems she did in class. She'd publish the classwork from the smartboard too. Her students loved it. The School Board did as well, and gave her multiple awards and even some additional funding to continue her work.

When Margot retired, she got letters and emails from former students thanking her for her work. She was that kind of teacher. But it was time for a new chapter in life.

The summer before she decided to retire, two parents of former students had contacted her independently about building a website for their businesses. One a dentist with a small practice and another a financial advisor, both had seen how well Margot's blog was put together, and decided to ask for her help.

The projects went pretty well, all things considered. Margot had never built a website for a business before, but she knew WordPress and found lots of help at her local meetup, in some WordPress Facebook groups, and on YouTube. Before the summer was over, she had launched both websites and had two happy clients. But more than that, Margot absolutely loved the work. And now she was ready to build a business for the second half of her life.

But today she was late. Almost 10 minutes late. Jason was about to close the video conference when Margot's face popped on the other half of the screen, apologizing repeatedly.

"Jason, I'm so sorry. You know me. I'm never late for anything."

"Relax Margot, what's going on?"

"Well, honestly, I just ended the worst client call of my life. And I'd include all the irate and snarky parents I've dealt with in my years of teaching too."

"Sounds pretty serious, tell me about it."

"I picked up this client a few months ago from one of my financial planner clients as a referral. He's a financial planner too. I have a few of them now. I think they like the fact that I was a math teacher." They both laughed. "But things went off the rails pretty quickly."

"How so?"

"Well, everything was urgent all of a sudden. It had to be done right away. And I don't think this guy knows what a period is. He ends every sentence with an exclamation point."

"Oh wow."

"And nothing seems to be right for this guy: not the design, not the copy, not even the colors. And he gave me the colors himself! He complains about everything, even when I've done exactly what he asked me to do. It's like he doesn't even remember the conversation."

"Did he start out this way or did he change into this other person at some point?"

"Well, I don't think he did. But then again, I was so excited to get a new client, I may have overlooked it. Come to think of it, we did spend a long time in our first meeting talking about the last web developer he worked with and how he couldn't get anything right. Now I'm starting to think that maybe he wasn't the problem. The client was."

"Margot, I think you've met a Drama Queen. Or, I guess, a Drama King in this case."

"Well, drama pretty well sums it up. I had enough drama dealing with junior high school students. I definitely don't need anymore."

"I can appreciate that. But now that you have Drama in your camp, the most important thing you can do is to document everything. You used to be required to keep documentation on students if there was an issue, right?"

"Did we ever. That was a must. Any time

there was a behavioral issue or contact with the parents, we had to document everything that happened. To be honest, I haven't missed it much."

"I wouldn't miss it either, but those skills are going to come in handy when you're dealing with a client like this. Actually, it's helpful to get used to documenting decisions with every client. Earlier, you said that he changed his mind about decisions you made together. Where did you have those conversations? By phone? Email?"

"No, he likes to meet in person. He basically insists on it. It's such a waste of time. We could talk by phone or video chat so much easier."

"Face to face meetings can be good. Misunderstandings don't happen nearly as often in face to face meetings. But I understand what you mean about the time commitment. Here's the problem, with this kind of client and face to face meetings. If you verbally agree to something, there's no record, no email trail you can point to if he decides to change his mind."

"You're exactly right, and that's a problem."

"So how did you document meetings with parents when you were teaching?"

"We had a form that summarized the meeting and any action steps needed for us to take or by them. They'd get a copy, I'd keep a copy, and one copy would go in a file with the Assistant Principal."

"And why was that important?"

"Well, that way it was clear that all the parties were on the same page. There was no misunderstanding of what actions were expected from anyone."

"Exactly. You should use the same kind of strategy with your clients. Whether they're Drama Kings, Drama Queens, or just an average person. Whenever you make a decision about something verbally, or in any meeting where there are action items for you or them, follow up with an email after the meeting summarizing the decisions and the action items everyone agreed to and who owns them."

"Like taking minutes of the meeting?"

"Well, not quite so formal or exhaustive. But more along the lines of Dear Mr. Client. Thanks for taking the time to meet with me today about how we will handle shipping methods and taxes on your website. As we discussed, you will meet with your accountant who should provide you with the taxes you are legally required to collect. And you will send this information to me, along with the shipping charges you want to collect based on the order totals..."

"That's perfect. It makes a lot of sense, and it will be easy to do."

"It really is. It becomes second-nature after a while. And the good thing is, should there ever be an issue, written communication is referenceable. You can point back to that email that documented the decision you made together."

"I will start doing that for every client immediately."

"Good start! The other thing to keep in mind with this kind of client is to stick to your guns when they pressure you. And they will pressure you. Your Drama King may throw a fit worthy of a second grader. Stay calm and keep referring back to your system and your process."

"What do you mean exactly?"

"System trumps drama. You've put together a solid system over the last year."

"With your help, yes. I feel good about it."

"When a client like this wants to kick his way out of the system that you use to work projects, you need to calmly but firmly hold him to the commitments he made when he signed your contract and agreed to work with you. Don't get emotional. Just stick to the facts. He really has no argument, other than he doesn't like what he committed to."

"I can do that. I was a fun teacher, but plenty of my students who tried to test me realized soon enough that I have a backbone of steel. I don't bend that easily."

"And that's exactly what you'll need when you're dealing with a client like this one."

"Here I thought I'd left all of the nonsense behind me when I left teaching."

"Not hardly. The common denominator here is that you're dealing with people and human nature. Anytime you deal with people, there are going to be problems. Our challenge as business owners is to create a structure for projects that keeps human nature in check and projects on track."

Margo nodded in agreement.

"Ok, one last question on this before we move on... What do you take away from this situation? It's important not to waste an experience with a bad client. We always need to learn from it and improve our systems wherever possible. How do you think you could avoid a client like this in the future?"

Margot thought for a minute. "In hindsight, I think the first red flag should have been when he spent so much time complaining about how the last web developer he worked with couldn't get anything right. But somehow I just assumed that it was all that other developer's fault and that I'd be able to come up with a solution he'd be happy with."

"I'm glad you said that, because that's exactly what I was going to suggest also. Now, given, there are a lot of knuckle-headed web developers out there. They don't listen to clients, and they do some really strange work. I've seen it all."

"Exactly, I've gotten a lot of work that way. Someone hired a developer who didn't know what he or she was doing, and I inherit a mess that needs fixing."

"That's what I call Rescue Work, and I've done my fair share too. But as soon as a potential client starts complaining about a previous web developer who did everything wrong, it's a full stop. I'm going to ask a lot of questions and dig into what they mean. I want to be sure that I'm dealing with a situation where they hired a poor developer, and that I'm not dealing with a Drama Queen."

"So how do you dig into that situation? What do you ask?"

"I just ask them to tell me the story. Why was the work unacceptable? And keep asking questions until we get to the heart of the matter. And I always ask them what could have changed to have made the previous project a success. If they take none of the blame themselves, it's a huge red flag."

"I like that. Asking questions is so important. Asking the right questions, I should say."

"So, what's your next step with this client?"

"I think I'm going to ask for another meeting where we look at where the project is based on what we agreed on at the beginning in the scope of work that he signed."

"Bring the signed contract with you and look at the words on the page. It's hard to argue with black and white."

"Good idea. Then we'll need to come up with a plan for getting the rest of the site completed with action items for each of us."

"And make sure to…"

"And make sure to email him afterward with a summary of the meeting and what we've each agreed to do."

"You got it."

"I feel pretty good about this now. He's going to be tough to deal with, but I think we can still get the project finished. Now, let me tell you about the site my sister wants me to build for her new business."

"Wait, you want to avoid drama, and you're going to work with family? This might require another call..."

They both laughed. "Maybe so."

PART TWO:

BUILDING FENCES AROUND FRIENDLY MONSTERS

INTRODUCTION

I am a passionate advocate for freelancers and business owners. I believe that real freedom comes from owning your own business, being in control of your time, your life and your priorities.

But over the years, I've encountered a sad reality. Through hundreds of conversations with freelancers, solopreneurs and agency owners across the country and around the world, I've found that many are just one bad client away from throwing in the towel. And it's a shame because virtually all client problems can be mitigated or eliminated by consistent systems and processes.

Clients are friendly monsters.
And every client has the potential
for transformation.

Have you ever been sitting in your first meeting with a client and everything is going well? You're thinking how great it will be working with this client. You imagine how amazing the final product will be. You say to yourself, "This is the perfect client." Two weeks into the project, your perfect client transforms into another person entirely. It's a total Dr. Jekyll and Mr. Hyde change.

Even friendly monsters
have teeth.

As business owners, we need to build fences around these friendly monsters or we will allow them to run free and trample the rest of our world. We'll waste time, money and (most importantly) emotional capitol dealing with the damage that these friendly monsters will cause.

Have you ever said things you regret to your spouse, or snapped at your kids because you were frustrated with a problem client? A single bad client can wreak emotional havoc on the rest of your life.

We need good fences to keep these monsters contained.

In this part of the book, I'm going to suggest four fences we need to build to deal with friendly monsters. And each of these fences is an integral part of a business system – a consistent set of processes that you use for every client, every project, every time.

The Importance of a System for your Business

Take a hard look at your current business model. Do you have a consistent system that you use for all your clients?

I'll let you in on a little secret… Most people who are building websites for clients are winging it. They have some things they do, mostly out of habit. Most do not have a consistent process that every client project must follow.

Don't believe the lie that because you're doing "custom work" you can't have a consistent system. I've been building custom websites for clients since 1995. Today, every single project follows the same process.

When you start to bring consistency into your business, you start to find something amazing. Consistency yields efficiency. When you run each of your client projects through the same process every time, you get better. You get faster. You innovate. Projects start to take less time to complete because you're following a consistent process.

BONUS: problem clients are contained within your system.

Sounds great right?

The Four Fences

In order to keep problem clients contained, we need to implement a system that includes these four strategies, which we'll call our fences:

1. Clarity
2. Commitments
3. Communication
4. Documentation.

There are many ways to create systems based on those four fences. My goal in this part of the book is to explain the concepts behind them and offer some practical suggestions on how you might implement them. Then, you can begin the work of integrating them into the unique way that you run your business.

There is no one right way to run a web business. But if you don't have these fences deeply ingrained into how your business works, you're going to have problems.

And you must have all four. If you're missing a fence, the friendly monsters will walk right out. And if one of your fences is weak, there will be certain kinds of clients who will exploit that weakness and create havoc in your world.

CLARITY
THE FIRST FENCE

Agreement does not equal clarity.

Differing expectations can derail a project and complicate your business.

A common mistake that freelancers make is to confuse agreement with clarity. It is possible for a client to agree to something verbally or in writing when they don't fully understand what they're agreeing to. This will be especially true when it comes to technical matters, you can have agreement without clarity.

We can complicate things by using technical jargon that muddies the water. Sometimes you may find that a client will simply agree to avoid the embarrassment of looking unintelligent. The client doesn't want to admit they don't understand the technical terms you're using.

It's our job as web professionals to be as

clear as possible when talking to the client, particularly when it comes to technical matters. Make it your mission to de-jargonize your speech when you're dealing with a client. Explain things at the most basic level. Focus on the end result using their perspective and what it means to them practically.

Sometimes we struggle with clarity because the client (innocently or not) doesn't tell us everything. More than once, I've dealt with a project in which the client did not volunteer key information that made a significant difference later in the project.

When that kind of situation happens, whose fault is that? I'd suggest that it's at least half and half. As professional web developers, we need to become masters at the soft skill of asking great questions in the initial meetings with the client. Like archaeologists, we need to dig through layer after layer until we unearth the truth. Keep asking how, why, and what until you uncover clarity.

This skill of asking great questions is one that will set you apart from other web developers.

Assumptions create confusion, not clarity.

Asking good questions is critical to root out what the client really needs. It's a thrill to see a light come on for the client as they are finally able articulate with clarity what they're looking for within the process. Without that kind of clarity, it's easy to suggest solutions that are based on our assumptions of client needs rather than what they actually need.

When we don't clearly explain the process we use to create websites, clients are left to make their own assumptions. Not good.

What is the client assuming that you will do?

What are you assuming the client will do?

All these assumptions will ultimately collide at some point during the project. And it's never pretty.

Be specific to create clarity.

Start by creating a list of intake questions that you ask about every project when you meet with a client for the first time. This could be a web form on your site or a checklist that you talk through when you're meeting face to face or on the phone.

When it comes to intake questions, don't wing it! If you try to ask these questions from memory, it's very likely you'll forget something. And in my experience, the question you forget to ask is often the question that needs to be asked the most.

Make a checklist and use it.

If you sense from your client's answers that you haven't reached clarity, keep probing until you find it. It will be obvious when you get there.

One of the most common places where assumptions are found is in the client's expectations of the work you'll actually be doing for them. That's why a clear scope of work is critical in your proposal. You want there to be no misunderstanding about what services you're providing for the price you provide.

Your contract is also one of the most important places where you can establish clarity with the client and remove any assumptions from the project.

A good contract isn't just legalese. It's a clear explanation of how your process for designing websites works. It explains what you're expecting your clients to do and what they can expect you to do.

Be crystal clear in your wording so that no assumptions linger. Do this, and if things go off the rails later, you can point back to the clear wording in your contract that the client signed.

Clarity in Action

We saw clarity in action as Carlos struggled with the Invisible Man. He needed to have clarity in his contract about what happens when a project is delayed by the client. It's critical to have language outlining how a project becomes suspended after a specified time if the client doesn't communicate, provide assets, or approve mile stones.

This is just one example of how clarity in your contract can help build fences around your friendly monsters. Every step in your process should have similar clarifying statements in your contract that explain what the client can expect from you, what you're expecting from them, and what happens if expectations aren't met.

Over the years I've learned that my contract is never finished – it's a work in progress. Occasionally, I will add new sections or modify existing ones based on the behavior and feedback of clients.

Friendly monsters rarely escape my fences these days, but when they do, it's time to strengthen them by tweaking my processes and contract language.

COMMITMENTS
THE SECOND FENCE

All healthy relationships are based on healthy commitments.

It took a long time for me to learn that. For years, I never thought about the client relationship in terms of a reciprocal commitment. In my mind, the client was giving me a check (usually a pretty small check) for something I loved to do, so I'd do whatever was necessary to get the site built and launched.

That may sound good at the first read, but it's a terrible way to run a business. You can't create a website for an individual or an organization without their input. When the client hires you, you're inviting him or her into a mutual relationship that is necessary to create their website.

The client has to be as committed to the project as you are – and that's more than just writing a check.

The client needs to have clarity on the commitments you're going to ask them to make throughout the project. It's important to emphasize these commitments both verbally and in writing in your contract.

And don't just explain it once. Explain the process throughout your interactions with the client.

I've learned over the years that you can tell some clients the same thing 100 times, but some clients just don't stay told.

Commitments in Action

We saw the importance of commitments as Theresa encountered the Question Mark. In her eagerness to get a new client, she invested hours of her time without ever getting any kind of commitment back from her in return. If you're like most people working with clients, you've encountered that situation before. And it's frustrating.

I remember one time in particular where I spend more than 2 hours at a coffee shop talking through a full ecommerce strategy with a potential client. I gave him advice about how to structure his pricing, how to tackle shipping and fulfillment, and how to handle sales tax. I did it for free, all for the privilege of writing a proposal… which he never responded to.

The gap between what you know
and what your client knows
has value.

Don't be afraid to charge for it.

I gave my client hundreds of dollars of value with no reciprocal commitment from him. Later I discovered that he took that insight I had so generously provided and hired a friend of his college-aged son to build the website on the cheap.

Lesson learned.

I resolved never again to provide that much value without compensation. And it was from that experience that I developed the rule of thumb I still use and teach today to help determine what questions to answer for free in an initial consultation:

> *"What" questions are usually free– they're informational.*
>
> *"How" questions usually cost money – they get into intellectual property.*

Nine Phases of Commitment

From the start, your process should have opportunities for clients to commit at key points.

Like any growing relationship, your work with clients is really a series of commitments that build upon each other. My process has nine phases, each dependent upon a commitment the client is asked to make along the way.

Phase 1: First Contact

In the first conversation with the client, the goal is to find out very briefly what kind of project they are interested in, and how they heard about you. Be clear about the minimum price for the kind of work they're asking for (brochure site, ecommerce, etc.), and that the minimum price is only a starting point depending on the features they request.

This first contact call usually lasts 5-10 minutes. No longer. When the client understands *and accepts* the minimum price then schedule the longer, initial consultation.

It's not uncommon to find yourself spending hours with the client talking about a project before the client has made any commitment whatsoever around scope and price. It's a great way to waste a lot of time.

Phase 2: Initial Consultation

This is the hour-long meeting where you will go deeper into the complexities of the project. You want to learn enough about the project to offer a proposal.

Ask the client at the beginning for their permission to run the meeting and explain about the list of questions to thoroughly examine what they want and start to consider the best way to accomplish their goals.

This is not a time for the client to dream about possibilities or ask a million questions.

At the end of the meeting, you should have enough information to give the client a ballpark price within a $1000 range.

I'll say something like this... *Based on what*

we've talked about today, we could create the website you've described for between $5500-$6500. If I return a proposal to you tomorrow that falls within that price range, are you ready to start the project?

"Are you ready to start the project?" is a soft close. The soft close is essential. Proposals can be a lot of work to assemble, especially for larger projects. You've already given the client more than an hour of your time at no cost (considering the initial contact and this first meeting). So, before you spend any more time on a proposal, you want to be sure they are committed to a ballpark price.

Phase 3: Proposal and Contract

Once the client agrees to the ballpark price, it's time to create a proposal and present it to them along with the contract.

I can't emphasize enough the importance of actually presenting the proposal to the client – face to face whenever possible. Don't rely on a nicely formatted PDF or an online proposal presentation website to do your selling for you.

Documents don't sell, you do.

The ball is in the client's court now. You are

asking for the biggest commitment yet – payment for the first half of the project, and their signature on two legal documents. Once they provide these items, you can start the project itself.

Phase 4: Content

One of the most important changes I've made to my process was moving to a *Content First* approach. For years, I would get the content piecemeal from the client. Some text here, a few pictures there. It took forever to build the site this way.

Now, as soon as we receive the deposit and signed documents from the client, we immediately create a Content Guide that will help the client assemble the content we'll need to create the website.

We don't do anything else on the project until we receive the Content Guide back 100% complete. That includes all the assets (photos, video, and other files) needed to create the website.

At this point, the client has made three huge commitments on the project:

1. Payment
2. Documents
3. Content

Now it's time for to get to work.

Phase 5: Design

It's time for a mockup of the website home page. At this stage, you are trying to nail down the colors, typography, design elements. You want the client to be satisfied that how the website looks. Have the client sign off on the design before you proceed with any development.

The rationale for a design sign-off is to prevent the client from coming back at the end of the project and making design-related changes. Design changes at the end of a project can take a long time to manage when they can be simple to make at the graphic level. This is why I get design sign-off before development.

If the client wants to make a change to something that was previously accepted, there will be hourly charges for the additional work that is required.

Coach's Tip:

It's a mistake to try to do design before you have the content for the site in full.

Design problems are usually content problems.

It's much easier to create a design to showcase

the content rather than try to shoehorn content into an existing design.

Your website will also be a lot more effective in presenting the information.

Phase 6: Development

Once the client approves the design, you can render it into a WordPress website. Add the content and assets the client provided in the Content Phase and populate the new site. Phase 6 is all about what you can do. There's no need for the client to sign off in this step.

Phase 7: Review and Testing

Time to get the client's perspective. After the website is completed, grant the client access for review and testing. It's always important to walk clients through the major sections of the website, reminding them of their goals for the website and explaining why you made the decisions you did in the website build to achieve those goals. Once the client is satisfied with the website, have the client sign off, and it's time to launch.

Phase 8: Launch

The launch process begins by collecting the remaining balance due for the project. That's the client's last big commitment for the project. Once the client supplies this, you can run your launch checklist and launch the website.

Phase 9: Management

A big part of my business is providing WordPress management services to my clients. It's a critical source of recurring revenue that balances out the feast or famine project cycle that most of us are all too familiar with as freelancers. The client commits to a monthly recurring credit card charge, and I provide management services to keep the new website healthy and secure.

Coach's Tip:

In my >ADVANCE Process course, this system is explained in more detail. Also included is my proposal and contract templates based on the same ones I use in my business today.

For more information, visit https://nathaningram.com/courses.

COMMUNICATION
THE THIRD FENCE

"The single biggest problem
in communication is the
illusion that it has taken place."

- George Bernard Shaw

As with many quotes on the Internet, there's some doubt as to whether Shaw said it. But there's no doubt that whoever said it is exactly right. Think for a moment about a misunderstanding you've had with a significant other.

The chances are that, regardless of the specific issues involved, much of the problem came from the style of communication (or lack of communication) that surrounded it. It's in the word itself: mis-*understanding*.

Communication is a complicated process that involves taking a concept from your mind and delivering it to someone else's mind with as little distortion as possible. When you consider the differences we all have with language, background, culture and preferences, it's a wonder we can communicate at all. Sometimes we really blow it.

When it comes to the client relationship, communication is something that we have to get right. I've learned along the way that good communication throughout the process of a project can make all the difference in the world.

Few things can improve the client's experience more than clear, regular communication.

Along with asking great questions, communication is one of those soft skills that, when properly developed, can set you apart from other web developers. Clients want to hear from you, even if it's just to update them on the status of their work.

The problem is that many web developers are not good communicators, and those who are often fail to prioritize it.

This is especially true when we've hit a snag and the project is stuck, maybe because we are struggling with a technical issue. Most of us have encountered a situation like that. It's not uncommon for there to be a few of these in every project.

Be honest. If you're stuck like this on a project, do you tend to communicate with the client or avoid them?

Most of us to hide in a cave and hope the client doesn't call. The last thing we want to do is have to explain to the client that we've encountered a technical problem. For some reason, we think that the client will lose all faith in us and cancel the project. So, we sit in the dark, hoping the phone won't ring. Or worse, we stop returning calls or emails.

Without regular communication, clients make assumptions – and they usually assume the worst.

That's human nature. In an information vacuum, our minds tend to rush to the worst possible explanation. It's important to communicate (and even overcommunicate) when things don't go as expected.

If you're afraid that communicating bad news will drive the client away, let me assure you that this will rarely be the case. In almost 25 years of working with clients building projects for the web, I've never had a single client withdraw because I had to deliver bad news. Not once.

There are plenty of other WordPress professionals out there the client could have hired to build their website, but they chose to hire you. The client hired you (most likely) because they like you and they trust you. There's no need to walk on eggshells. In fact, my experience has taught me that if you communicate bad news to the client in a professional way, you actually strengthen trust and build the relationship.

Just don't go break something so you can build trust. That's not how it works.

Communication in Action

We saw the importance of putting good boundaries around communication in Sean's experience with the Boundary Buster. When you're dealing with any client, it's important to clearly communicate how and when you work.

One of the frequent mistakes that freelancers make is believing that they have to be available at the whim of the client. In the early days of my business, it was not uncommon for me to pull myself away from family events or hobbies to take a phone call from a client that would often sidetrack the rest of the day.

I did it in the name of good customer service. And I was wrong. It's ok to explain that you only work during normal business hours and let those calls go to voicemail.

Email is another story.

Say you're sitting in bed or on the couch one evening casually watching television or doing something on your phone. Then you receive a notification that a new email has come in. Out of habit, you open your inbox where you find a short email from a client asking a question. It will only take 20 seconds to reply. What do you do?

If you're like I was for years, you open the email, shoot off a quick response, and pat yourself on the back for great customer service. You answered the client's email at 10pm. And you go to sleep thinking it's a good thing.

But in reality, what have you done? You've just communicated to the client that she can expect to receive immediate responses to after-hours email. You've just fed the Mogwai after midnight. You've created a monster.

I use an email app that allows me to delay the sending of emails until a date and time that I specify. Even if I choose to respond to an email after hours, I delay it to send until the next day. I frequently delay sending emails throughout the day as well so that clients and others who email me don't begin to expect immediate responses.

When it comes to communication, remember that actions speak louder than words.

The Friday Email Strategy

One way to ensure good communication is happening throughout a project, whether the news is good or bad, is by implementing the Friday Email Strategy.

I send a weekly email on Friday afternoons to every active project I'm working on. Each client gets an email that has a status update in 3 simple sentences. Think of them in terms of past, present, and future.

Sentence One: Past
This is the work that was accomplished on your project this week.

Sentence Two: Present
This is where things stand today in terms of the project as a whole.

Sentence Three: Future
This is the work we'll be doing next week.

Then, invite any questions or comments from them and wish them a great weekend. (Technically makes four sentences, but you get the idea).

That's it!

Simple right? But when every client with an active project gets an email like this every week, people tend to stay on the same page. And believe me, the clients love it.

An example Friday email after a good week:

SUBJECT: Weekly Project Status Update

Dear Michael,

This week I worked on getting several of the pages of your website built, including your About Us page, Team Members page, Locations pages, and Contact page.

The website is nearly complete and is on schedule to launch in two weeks as planned.

Next week I will finish the remaining pages and send the site to you for review (watch your email for a link).

As always, should you have any questions in the meantime, please reach out.

Have a great weekend!
Nathan

The Friday email is also the place to explain when you've encountered an unexpected problem. There's no need to go into the details, just give the client a status update and how things stand regarding the project as a whole and what impact, if any, the problem might have on an estimated launch date if it exists. There's no need to overshare, just explain.

An example Friday email explaining a problem:

SUBJECT: Weekly Project Status Update

Dear Sherry,

This week I've been working on getting your products added to the ecommerce system and all the settings working for shipping costs and payments. Unfortunately, I had some problems getting the shipping costs to calculate correctly and pull live rates from USPS.

I am in communication with the developers of the USPS connector, and I anticipate that we will have the issue solved early next week. I will do my best to make up for the lost time, but this problem might delay the estimated launch of your website by a few days.

Next week I will be working to bring a final solution to the problem and then begin working on the informational pages of the website.

As always, should you have any questions in the meantime, please reach out.

Have a great weekend!
Nathan

The example above has a couple of extra sentences to explain the problem. But also notice that, although the issue was explained, it was not unpacked entirely.

In most cases, the client doesn't need to know all the details. They just want to know what's going on. And it's much better to explain that there might be a short delay here in the middle of the project than waiting to tell them until the last minute.

The Friday email is also the place to remind the client that you're waiting on content or assets from them before you can move forward on the project. It's also the place to explain where they stand in terms of a suspended project clause in your contract, if you have one of those.

An example Friday email when the project is on hold waiting on an approval from the client:

Dear Allison,

This week I was unable to do any work on your website project because I am still waiting to receive your feedback or approval for the design concept that was sent to you two weeks ago.

I cannot proceed to the development stage, in which your website is actually built, until the design concept has been approved. The delay will also affect the estimated launch date of your website accordingly.

If I do not receive feedback or approval by the end of next week, I will have to suspend your project and take it out of my active workflow. As explained in my Master Services Agreement, to reactivate a suspended project, your approval or feedback on the design and payment in full for the remainder of the project will be required.

Should you have any questions about this process, or if we can assist you with the process of offering feedback on the design, please reach out.

Have a good weekend!
Nathan

That's never a fun email to send, but the Friday email is an excellent place to communicate a tough message like that.

There's no need for overcommunicating or arm-twisting. Just point the client to the commitments they made in the contract when they hired you. Don't be afraid to hold them accountable.

Coach's Tip:

I've observed over the years that
the longer a project takes, the more likely
the project is to go off the rails.

As time passes, especially in the
absence of regular communication,
clients will tend to forget the
commitments they previously made.

So, if you're dealing with a delay, be sure that you ramp up the communication so that you can maintain clarity throughout the project.

By the way, it's never too late to start a communication strategy. Don't wait until the next project to start. If you're reading this and realize that your communication has been lacking, start now on your existing projects.

Increasing communication is also an effective way to deal with a project that's currently delayed, especially if you tend to go silent when you're frustrated. Start sending those Friday emails, and you might be surprised how you can get a stuck project moving again.

DOCUMENTATION
THE FOURTH FENCE

There's no other way to say this: documentation may be boring, but it can also save you from a client nightmare.

If you don't document, you're relying on your own memory – or worse, the client's memory.

When you're dealing with clients, get used to communicating in writing. It's a habit that isn't difficult to start, but it's one that you won't regret.

The first time you're able to point back to an email follow-up where you and the client made a decision that the client didn't remember, you'll see how critical the skill of documentation can be.

If you're anything like me, you have lots of verbal meetings with your clients. For me, that's part of the value I bring. My clients appreciate meeting with someone accessible and local who will talk them through the complexities of accomplishing their goals on the web and do it in plain language.

The problem with verbal meetings, whether in person or by voice or video, is that no one is taking minutes. If a decision is made during a verbal meeting, and later you and your client have a different recollection of the decision, you're in trouble.

Documentation in Action

Margot learned the importance of documentation when she met the Drama Queen. But no matter what kind of client you're dealing with, documenting everything is critical. Unfortunately, this is frequently the fence that gets neglected the most.

Make a habit of communicating in writing. Written communication is referenceable.

I'm not suggesting that you abandon verbal meetings with the client, but I recommend adding one more step to the process. After the meeting is over, send a quick email to the client summarizing your meeting notes (you are taking notes during all your meetings, right?).

Your email should briefly describe any decisions that were made and action items that were assigned.

An example follow-up email from a client meeting:

Dear Allen,

Thanks for taking the time to meet today about the changes you would like to make to your website. This email is a quick summary of what we decided.

Since your events are much less frequent today than when the site was built, we decided to remove the events calendar and start using blog posts to promote your events instead.

You agreed to take the information for your four active events and add them as blog posts with featured images.

Once this is finished, I will create an events category for these and future event posts, and add an area on your home page where these events will display.

We agreed that the cost for this work would be $375.

Should you have any questions about these things, as always, just reach out.

Thanks again for your continued trust in me as your website manager,

Nathan

That email should take you less than 3 minutes to type and send. But, if for some reason there is a misunderstanding between you and the client about what you agreed to in that meeting, it will be the best 3 minutes you'll spend this week.

The details of the meeting are summarized and referenceable just in case there is any misunderstanding. And if, in the worst-case scenario, you reach a point with a client where legal action is required, you have a summary of your interactions that can be used to support your claims in court, even if the client didn't respond to the message.

One final note on documentation of decisions… The approval of any project phase should always be in writing. If I'm meeting with the client and she gives a thumbs up to the design I present, I always ask her to send a quick email stating her approval of the design as presented today.

You always want to have an email for reference in case things go haywire in the future.

Implement a system that can easily capture all project communication.

There isn't one solution for this that is right for everyone. I know many successful web developers who are all using very different tools to capture project communication.

Today there are many options: Basecamp and Teamwork, Evernote and One Note, Trello and Asana, and many, many choices for CRMs. Depending on your personal preferences and how you want to structure the internals of your business, any of these could be the right solution for you.

The best solution is the one that you will use consistently.

There is a character trait that you and I probably share. It's common among those of us who self-identify as geeks (a term I use with affection). We tend to look at a problem like an information management system and spend weeks and months researching to find the best possible solution. Or worse, try to build one ourselves.

We'll create some elaborate thing. We'll tinker and fiddle. We'll spend countless hours. We'll use it religiously for a week… *and then never touch it again.*

When it comes to this system to manage project information, don't overthink it. Find something you will be able to use consistently and then just use it. It's never going to be perfect. But any of the solutions I mentioned will do the job well enough.

CONCLUSION:

DON'T TEAR DOWN YOUR FENCES

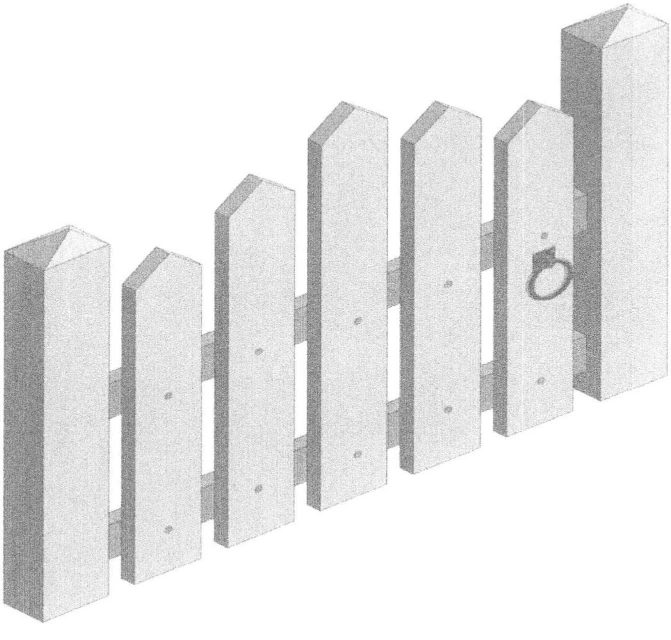

The Biggest Mistake

Hopefully, through the process of reading this book, you've been able to identify some key strategies that you can use to improve the client side of your business. Maybe you've recognized some of the friendly monsters because you have dealt with them first-hand. And maybe you'll be more likely to identify them more quickly in the future before they trample the rest of your life.

But as I bring this book to a close, it's important that I share with you the biggest mistake I repeatedly see when it comes to building fences around friendly monsters. I've heard it in countless conversations with WordPress business owners around the world. And I've seen it in my own life and business.

We tend to spend lots of time and effort building the fences around our businesses. We understand how important they are. Then it comes time for the fences to be put to the test.

One day a client will come along and break a rule. And then they'll want you to make an exception. You'll feel a strong push to give in. Or maybe, the client will break a rule and you want to "be nice" (which is code for avoiding confrontation), so you choose not to hold the client accountable.

You might start to generate excuses for the client in your mind. You might even fool yourself into thinking that giving in or not holding them accountable is somehow "great customer service."

But after you pat yourself on the back for a little while, then something starts to happen inside. That feeling of accomplishment starts to curdle. Pretty soon it becomes a hint of resentment. "Why did they do that? They signed the contract, they knew my rules."

The more you dwell on it, that hint of resentment can turn into full-blown frustration. And by the end of the work day, you're angry. When you get home, you're snippy with your significant other. You fuss at the kids or the dog. You're not a fun person to be around. All because you let the client weasel out of a commitment he made.

Consider the insanity of this.

Instead of forcing a stranger to live with the consequences they've earned, we take it out on the people closest to us. We're nice to the client and mean to the people we love. It's crazy.

You spent the time to create systems and processes in your business. Every one of them is there for a reason.

Don't break your own rules.
Don't tear down your fences.

This is especially important if you are a "nice person." You can hold the client to his commitment and still be nice about it. Just stick to the facts.

And if you're a nice person, it's probably wise to find another freelancer or a close friend or a coach to become accountable to on this issue.

The Payoff

Building fences is hard work. Enforcing them can be even harder. But it's totally worth it. I can honestly say that it's been years since I had a problem client who wrecked my world. That's the result of identifying problem clients before they come in, but also holding clients accountable to the system I created.

What would your business be like if you had consistent processes that created strong fences?

Would you make more money?

Would you have less stress?

Would your work-life balance improve?

Yes, yes and yes.

So, get started! Implement the suggestions in this book and start building fences around friendly monsters.

NEED HELP?

Nathan has three courses designed to help WordPress professionals become more successful in their businesses.

Courses for WordPress Freelancers

Based on almost 25 years of experience owning and operating a web development business, learn how to avoid the common mistakes and blow up the obstacles in the way of your growth.

Learn more at nathaningram.com/courses.

>ADVANCE Process Course

Establishing systems for your business is one of the most important first steps a freelancer can take. Developing a consistent set of tools, processes, and checklists for every client, every project, every time is key. This course will give you a blueprint for success includes my proposal template and the contract that I use with clients.

> ADVANCE Profits Course

Being smart with your money is just as important as doing great work for your clients. In this course, we'll talk about developing a mindset for success, dialing in your pricing, charging what you're worth, and building recurring revenue.

>ADVANCE Productivity

As a WordPress business owner, your time is money. So, integrating habits into your workflow that help us manage time efficiently is critical. This course will provide you with a system to grow your business even while you're busy with client work.

Individual Coaching

Nathan is available on a limited basis for one on one and group coaching sessions.

Learn more at nathaningram.com/coaching.

The WP Business Podcast

Hosted by Nathan, this free podcast features WordPress industry news, helpful plugins and tools, and interviews focused on people who work with clients using WordPress.

Learn more at mywpbusiness.com.

ABOUT THE AUTHOR

Nathan Ingram is a WordPress educator, business coach, and host of the WP Business Podcast. He is a keynote speaker at WordPress events, and travels frequently to WordCamps internationally.

Nathan has been creating websites for clients since 1995 and is still actively building and managing WordPress websites.

Nathan has been married to Monie since 1994. They live in Birmingham, Alabama with their two teenage daughters and two spoiled dogs.

To learn more, see Nathan's speaking schedule or engage Nathan for speaking or consulting, visit nathaningram.com.

Made in the USA
Monee, IL
14 January 2023

25245104R00066